# LADIES' NIGHT OUT

BY ALLISON KENT
AND BRIAN L. PELLHAM

Edited by Sally Neary
Cover Art by Wayne Merchant
Artwork by Steve Sindiong

Special thanks to Chris Bierrum, Samantha Cross, Mimi
Fontenelle, Mark Gustafson, May Gustafson, Jennifer Howe,
Tricia Kent, Nick Kokkonis, Kathy Megano, Natashia Nicolay,
Christopher Obert, Clara Pellham, Tony Pellham, Sean
Pohtilla, Emily Ross, Jessica Ross, Russell Scherer, Carbinos
Simien, Kelly Ward, and Quanchesca Ward for their
contributions.

*Inquiries should be addressed to*
WildPartyGames.com
1153 NW 51st Street
Seattle, WA 98107

inquiries@wildpartygames.com

DEDICATED TO
CHRIS AND JESSICA

# ABOUT THE AUTHORS

Always a bridesmaid and never the bride. While some women bemoan this fact, Allison Kent has made a career of it. Well... maybe just a part-time career on the weekends with no pay, but a rewarding endeavor nonetheless. Allison Kent is a games expert and co-author of *Outrageous Party Games*. Inventing games and event planning are much treasured hobbies for her. She spends her Saturday nights... yep, you guessed it..... out on the

town, hitting the bars, and partying it up in the name of research.

Allison's co-author, Brian L. Pellham, doesn't know a damn thing about women. He is, however, one of the country's most renowned experts on drinking and party games (if there is such a thing). To date, he has invented over 200 romance and party games, including Passion Throw, the throw blanket love game; Beer!, the drinking card game; and Got Liquor?, a shot glass and drinking game set. Also, his first book *A Partier's Guide to 51 Drinking Games* has sold several hundred thousand copies. He spends his Saturday nights whittling knickknacks on his porch. (Life can't be all fun and games, you know.)

# TABLE OF CONTENTS

# CHOOSE YOUR OWN ADVENTURE
## (an Introduction)

Ladies' Night Out is a collection of classic and original party games that are designed specifically for women. We know that today's woman is busy and has many celebrations in life, which is why we designed Ladies' Night Out to be versatile.

The book begins with games to get the party started and encourage mingling among guests. As the book (and evening) progress, you can move the party to the bar, out on the town, or just kick it up a notch wherever you are. We have included drinking games, social games, and games that encourage your guest of honor to interact with handsome strangers. The final chapter is designed for the peak of the evening when your guests are feeling uninhibited, wild, and perhaps even a bit inebriated.

Give your guest of honor a night she can only hope to remember, with Ladies' Night Out!

# SYMBOLS

 = A prize should be offered to the winner(s).

 = There is a secret to this game. The rules should not be shared with the entire group.

 = You may wish to make photocopies of a sample list or game pieces when preparing to play this game.

 = This game is more suitable for bachelorette parties than other events.

 = This is a drinking game.

 = Personal information will be shared between players.

# GET THE PARTY STARTED

# THE NAME GAME

**Number of Players** 6+

## Supplies
- Adhesive name tags (or several sheets of paper and tape)
- A marker

## Setup
The hostess writes down the names of famous people on pieces of paper or adhesive name tags. She should write only one name per tag, and must generate enough names to provide each player with one. The hostess then attaches one tag to each player's back so that other players can view the name. Players should not be shown the names that have been taped to their own backs.

## Play
The object of the game is for players to correctly identify the names that have been placed on their backs. Players should consider the names to be assumed identities. They should pair off to ask each other yes/no questions in order to gather clues. Examples of appropriate questions are, "Am I an actress?" and "Do I play a leading role in a sitcom?" Players shouldn't ask more than three consecutive questions of the same player (unless there are only two players remaining in the game). Players may return to their previous partners to ask additional questions later in the game.

When a player thinks she has determined her famous identity, she should ask someone, "Is the name on my back (her guess)?" If she is correct, she should withdraw from the game. The other players continue playing, guessing, and exiting the game until there is only one player remaining.

The first player to identify the name on her back wins the game. She should be awarded a prize for this victory.

# THE BRIDAL QUIZ

**Number of Players** 6+

**Supplies**
- One piece of paper per player
- One pen or pencil per player

**Setup**

This game dares to ask the question, "How well do you really know the bachelorette?" To begin the game, players gather around the bachelorette, and each player is given a piece of paper and a writing utensil.

**Play**

The hostess reads a question aloud to the group from the Bridal Quiz Question List following this game. Each of the players records how she believes the bachelorette will answer the question. Once they are done recording their guesses, the bachelorette reveals her answer. Players who guess incorrectly are eliminated from the game. Players who answer correctly proceed to Round Two and the hostess poses another question to the bachelorette. If nobody is able to answer a question correctly, the question may be discarded at the discretion of the hostess. The game continues until only one player (besides the bachelorette) remains. A prize should be awarded to the winner.

# BRIDAL QUIZ QUESTION LIST:

1. At what age did the bachelorette lose her virginity?

2. What was the name of the bachelorette's first love?

3. Besides getting married, what is the most exciting thing that has happened to the bachelorette?

4. How many children would the bachelorette like to have?

5. Who is the bachelorette's least favorite ex-boyfriend?

6. What is the bachelorette's favorite movie?

7. Who is the bachelorette's favorite author?

8. What is the bachelorette's favorite "Boy" band?

9. How did the bachelorette meet her husband-to-be?

10. If the bachelorette was "forced" to have one final fling before tying the knot, whom would she choose?

# LIAR LIAR

## Number of Players  12+

## Supplies
- Three chairs
- A hat (or bowl)
- Two strips of paper per player
- Several pens or pencils

## Setup
The hostess places the three chairs at the front of the room facing the group. She assigns the role of moderator to one of the players who is familiar with all of the other players' names. Each player, except the moderator, writes her name and a true experience on each of the two strips of paper provided by the hostess. Players should choose unique, yet simple experiences. An example of an entry is, "I used to fantasize about my high school math teacher." The entries should be actual experiences of the players. The moderator collects all of the entries.

## Play
The moderator pulls an entry out of the hat and reads the experience aloud. Players who wish to participate in the round raise their hands. The participant whose entry was selected must raise her hand. The moderator then selects three players from the group of volunteers, including the author of the

selected entry. These players occupy the three seats at the head of the room. The moderator selects the order in which the participants present their tales.

The two participants who did not submit the experience fabricate a story, while the author of the entry tells the truth. The participants who devise fictitious stories for the round should try to convince the audience that they are telling the truth. Audience members may ask probing questions of each participant immediately following her explanation. After the third player has told her story and answered all questions, the moderator asks the audience to vote for the player they believe is telling the truth. Then the player who told the truth steps forward. This is the end of Round One.

Round Two begins when the moderator pulls another entry out of the hat. The game ends after ten rounds.

# FAMOUS PEOPLE

**Number of Players** 4+

## Supplies
- A piece of paper (for keeping score)
- A hat (or bowl)
- A two-minute timer
- Ten strips of paper per player
- Several pens or pencils

## Setup
Players divide themselves evenly into teams of two to five players. They write down the names of ten famous people individually on strips of paper provided by the hostess. Players may write down the names of movie stars, athletes, poets, or anyone else that they consider famous. A name may be obscure, but at least one of the other players should be able to verify that the person is famous (if the entry is contested). Players should not discuss their entries with other participants. Players fold completed entries and place them into the hat.

## Play
Player One begins by pulling a strip of paper from the hat. At the same time, a player from an opposing team starts the two-minute timer. Player One describes the famous person that she has selected to her team. As she offers clues to her teammates, they try to guess the famous person's name.

There are a few restrictions on the types of clues that may be given:

- Do not use words that rhyme with the name. For example, Player One draws the entry "Margaret Cho." She may not say, "The last name rhymes with Hoe."
- Do not say any part of the name, even if a player has already guessed a portion of it.
- Gestures are not permitted.

After her team correctly identifies the famous person, Player One pulls another name from the hat. Her turn continues until the time expires. She may not skip any of the names that she selects. When a famous person has been correctly identified, the entry should be set aside. If the last entry a player selects is not identified before the time expires, the entry should be returned to the hat. If Player One gives an inappropriate clue, the entry is discarded and she must draw a new name. She may contest obscure entries at the end of her turn. If no one else is familiar with the person, besides the author of the entry, she may forego her points and retake her turn.

Team One receives one point for each correct answer identified within the allotted time. The team loses a point for each name that was discarded.

After Team One's points have been tallied, it is Team Two's turn. Within a team, each player must take a turn as the clue provider before any player is permitted to give clues a second time.

The game ends when no more strips of paper remain in the hat. Whichever team has the most points when the names run out wins the game. Prizes should be awarded to members of the winning team.

# WHAT HAVE YOU DONE?

**Number of Players**  10+

**Supplies**
- A stopwatch (or clock)
- One list of actions per player
- One pen or pencil per player

**Setup**
The hostess selects one of the four lists that follow this game:
Formal Acquaintances, Social Friends and Acquaintances,
Risqué, and Bizarre.  She then makes enough copies to provide
each participant with her own list.  She distributes the copies
immediately before play begins.  The hostess does not collect
signatures or sign lists during the game.  Instead, she monitors
the time, collects and scores the completed lists, and addresses
any questions that arise.

**Play**
Players get to know one another better by locating people in
the group who have engaged in actions found on the list.  Once
the hostess starts the stopwatch, players begin mingling.  If
Player One admits to engaging in one of the listed activities,
Player Two should have Player One sign her name in the space
provided.  For larger groups of twenty or more people, players
should only be permitted to have each person's signature once

on their pages.  If the group is not large enough for this rule, players may have other players sign their lists more than once, but they should only collect one signature at a time.  For example, if Jan signs Marcia's list, Marcia must collect another signature before Jan may sign Marcia's list a second time.  Also, players are not permitted to sign their own lists.

The player who collects the most signatures and completes the list first (within the allotted time) submits her list to the hostess.  The hostess then reviews the list to make sure that it is complete and accurate.  Until the hostess announces a winner, players should continue to search for more matches.  If players cannot complete the list (i.e., if there are one or more items that no one has done), then the person who submits the most complete list after ten minutes wins the game.  A prize should be offered to encourage players to socialize more and complete their lists.

## FORMAL ACQUAINTANCES VERSION

Locate other players who have done the following:

Visited Africa _____

Been Bungee Jumping _____

Was a Cheerleader in High School _____

Fallen Asleep While Driving _____

Worked in a Fast Food Restaurant _____

Taken a Road Trip Across the U.S. _____

Belly Danced _____

Gone Skinny-Dipping _____

Parented More Than One Child _____

Modeled Professionally _____

Re-gifted a Present _____

## SOCIAL FRIENDS AND ACQUAINTANCES VERSION

Locate other players who have done the following:

Accidentally Started a Fire _____

Eaten Dinner at a Convenience Store _____

Slept in a Train Station _____

Been Arrested _____

Danced on Top of a Bar _____

Fallen Asleep While on a Date _____

Made Out in a Public Restroom _____

Thrown Up in Public _____

Drawn Graffiti _____

Viewed Every Episode of *Sex in the City* _____

Crashed a Party _____

## RISQUÉ VERSION

Locate other players who have done the following:

Slept With a Friend's Ex-Lover _____

Purchased a Vibrator _____

Romantically Kissed Someone 20 Years Older _____

Used Food While Making Love _____

Visited a Nudist Colony or Beach _____

Lied About Her Age to a Lover _____

Worn Handcuffs _____

Watched an Entire X-Rated Movie _____

Made Love in a Public Place _____

Worn Crotchless Underwear _____

Participated in a Three-Way _____

## BIZARRE VERSION

Locate other players who have done the following:

Attempted to Impersonate a Famous Person _____

Secretly Used a Friend's Toiletries _____

Pierced Something Below Her Neck _____

Dressed Up for the Rocky Horror Picture Show_____

Joined a Dating Service _____

Hocked Something _____

Dyed Hair Red, White, or Blue _____

Eaten Dinner Naked _____

Visited Someone in Prison _____

Trimmed a Bonsai Tree _____

Ridden a Mechanical Bull _____

# TV MADNESS

**Number of Players**  10+

## Supplies
- A stopwatch (or clock)
- One pen or pencil per player

## Setup
This game was designed to reward players who watch a lot of television.  The hostess selects a general character theme depicted in many situation comedies, soap operas, or evening dramas.  Examples of such character themes include famous television couples, villains, virgins, and crime-solving partners.  For more advanced players (also known as couch potatoes), offer more challenging classifications.

Based on the theme, the hostess assembles a list of character names that fit into the chosen topic.  The hostess arranges the list so that guests must identify characters' first names based on the limited amount of information she has provided.  For example, if she selects famous television rock groups as the theme, the list might include O-Town, the Partridge Family, and Menudo.  For this example, each of the musical groups should be listed next to the appropriate number of blank lines (one line per band member).  A sample list and answer key for Famous Television Couples follow this game.  After finishing the list, the hostess makes a copy for each guest.

**Play**

The hostess gives each player a copy of the list, specifies what information she is looking for, and instructs the guests to fill in the missing data. She informs the players that they have ten minutes to accomplish this task, and starts the timer.

Once time is up, the hostess collects the lists and scores them. Each correct answer is worth one point. She should not deduct points for incorrect answers. The player who provides the highest number of correct answers should be awarded a prize.

**Variation**

If the game is being played at a bridal shower, add the bride and groom's married name to the sample list.

# FAMOUS TELEVISION COUPLES

Fill in the first names of these popular television couples. You have ten minutes.

1. _____ and _____ Cleaver

2. _____ and _____ Keaton

3. _____ and _____ Simpson

4. _____ and _____ Jefferson

5. _____ and _____ Brady

6. _____ and _____ Romano

7. _____ and _____ Bunker

8. _____ and _____ Flintstone

9. _____ and _____ Montgomery

10. _____ and _____ Roper

11. _____ and _____ Howell

12. _____ and _____ Jetson

13. _____ and _____ Munster

14. _____ and _____ Ingalls

15. _____ and _____ Bundy

16. _____ and _____ Soprano

17. _____ and _____ Walsh

18. _____ and _____ Bing

19. _____ and _____ Huxtable

20. _____ and _____ Kramden

21. _____ and _____ Ricardo

22. _____ and _____ Cunningham

23. _____ and _____ Carrington

24. _____ and _____ Spencer

25. _____ and _____ Addams

26. _____ and _____ Connor

# FAMOUS TELEVISION COUPLES - ANSWER KEY

1. June and Ward Cleaver (Leave it to Beaver)
2. Elise and Stephen Keaton (Family Ties)
3. Marge and Homer Simpson (The Simpsons)
4. Louise and George Jefferson (The Jeffersons)
5. Carol and Mike Brady (The Brady Bunch)
6. Debra and Raymond Romano (Everybody Loves Raymond)
7. Edith and Archie Bunker (All in the Family)
8. Wilma and Fred Flintstone (The Flintstones)
9. Dharma and Greg Montgomery (Dharma and Greg)
10. Helen and Stanley Roper (Three's Company)
11. Lovey and Thurston Howell (Gilligan's Island)
12. Jane and George Jetson (The Jetsons)
13. Lilly and Herman Munster (The Munsters)
14. Caroline and Charles Ingalls (Little House on the Prairie)
15. Peg and Al Bundy (Married with Children)
16. Carmela and Anthony Soprano (the Sopranos)
17. Cindy and Jim Walsh (Beverly Hills 90210)
18. Monica and Chandler Bing (Friends)
19. Claire and Cliff Huxtable (The Cosby Show)
20. Alice and Ralph Kramden (The Honeymooners)
21. Lucy and Ricky Ricardo (I Love Lucy)
22. Marion and Howard Cunningham (Happy Days)
23. Krystal and Blake Carrington (Dynasty)
24. Laura and Luke Spencer (General Hospital)
25. Morticia and Gomez Addams (The Addams Family)
26. Roseanne and Dan Connor (Roseanne)

# HOLLYWOOD EVER AFTER

**Number of Players**  4+

## Supplies
- A two-minute timer
- Several pads of paper (for keeping score and recording each team's answers)
- Several pens or pencils

## Setup
The hostess divides players evenly into two teams and supplies each with a pad of paper and a writing utensil.

## Play
The game begins when the hostess describes the topic for the round that she has selected from the Topic List that follows this game.  The teams then have two minutes to compile lists with as many responses as they can think of that fit the topic.

At the end of each round, the teams take turns reading their answers aloud.  Teams are awarded one point for each correct answer they have listed.  If the opposing team has an identical answer, neither team receives a point and the answers are discarded.  Teams are not penalized for incorrect answers.

After each team's score has been tallied, the next round begins and the hostess reads a new topic aloud. Whichever team has the most points at the end of five rounds wins the game. Prizes should be awarded to members of the winning team.

# HOLLYWOOD EVER AFTER - Topic List

1. Movies with plots that revolved around a wedding.

2. These actors/actresses launched the career of a bad actor/ actress by marrying them.

3. Actors/Actresses who gave it all up for marriage.

4. Actors/Actresses who have been married more than three times.

5. Famous people who have married within the last year.

6. Hollywood couples who have made it work (enjoyed five or more years of marriage).

7. Famous television couples.

8. Television shows that ended (or fizzled out) when two of the leading characters finally got married.

# DRAMA QUEEN

## Number of Players  4+

## Supplies
- A pair of scissors
- A hat (or bowl)
- A two-minute timer
- A piece of paper (for keeping score)
- A pen or pencil

## Setup
In preparation for this game, the hostess should photocopy one of the lists of words that follow this game (the Standard Edition or the Wedding Edition).  She should then separate the words by cutting along the dashed lines.   This creates strips of paper that list three words ranging in difficulty from easy to hard.  The words on the left are more common and easier to perform, while the words on the right are more obscure.  The three words are related by a common theme.  The strips should be folded and placed in a hat or bowl.

Players divide themselves evenly into two teams.  Make sure that players have enough room to comfortably act out the clues when the game begins.

## Play

A player from Team One is selected to act out words for the first round. As soon as the timer has been flipped, the actress selects an entry at random from the hat. She then attempts to act out the first word listed on the entry for her team. The actress cannot give any verbal clues or write down any information, however, she may use objects in the room as props to assist her in conveying the clues to her team.

The actress's team must identify the first word listed on the entry before she is permitted to act out any subsequent words or select a new entry. She is allotted two minutes to act out entries. If the first word is identified before time expires, the team scores one point. After Team One guesses the first word, the actress may choose to perform the second word listed on the entry. If the actress thinks that it is too difficult a word to perform, or becomes frustrated after trying, she may discard the entry and draw a new one.

If Team One correctly identifies the second word on an entry within the allotted time, the team scores two more points. Then the actress may choose to act out the third word, which is worth three points if it is correctly identified. Otherwise, she may discard the entry and draw a new one. For each new entry that is drawn, the first word is worth one point, the second is worth two points, and the third is worth three points.

When time runs out, all used entries should be discarded, and the score for the turn is added to the team's total. If the opposing team is able to identify the word that was being performed when time expired, they are awarded one point. The opposing team is only allowed one guess when trying to steal the point. Next, Team Two designates a player to act out entries.

When Team Two finishes, Round One ends and Team One designates a new actress for the second round. All players on a team must take a turn acting out entries before any player is permitted to take a second turn.

The team with the most points when the entries run out wins.

# DRAMA QUEEN - Standard Edition

| Level 1 | Level 2 | Level 3 |
| --- | --- | --- |
| Sign Language | English | Pig Latin |
| Donate | Volunteer | Community Service |
| Dear Abby | Oprah | Martha Stewart |
| Hopscotch | Tag | Kick-the-Can |
| Yoga | Meditate | Soul Searching |
| Life | Death | Afterlife |
| Convertible | S.U.V. | Tractor |
| President | Senator | Governor |
| Fraternity | Library | Dormitory |
| Oscar | Grammy | Nobel Peace Prize |
| Video Games | Gameshows | Puzzles |
| Romance | Fairy Tale | Fiction |
| Alcohol | Caffeine | Nicotine |

| Level 1 | Level 2 | Level 3 |
| --- | --- | --- |
| Sugar | Candy Bar | Licorice |
| Hallucinate | War on Drugs | Crack Baby |
| Devil | Possessed | Exorcism |
| Embarrassment | Pride | Rage |
| Spandex | Velcro | Vinyl |
| Body Odor | Jock Itch | Acne |
| See-Through | Fatigues | Toga |
| Dog Catcher | Sheriff | Prison Guard |
| Tuxedo | Prom | Chaperone |
| Spell | Witchcraft | Harry Potter |
| Chimpanzee | Turtle | Pigeon |
| Fried Chicken | Hamburger | Taco |
| Soccer | Ice Hockey | Shuffle Board |
| Cash | Loan Shark | Bank |

# DRAMA QUEEN - Wedding Edition

| Level 1 | Level 2 | Level 3 |
|---------|---------|---------|
| First Kiss | Wedding Night | Virginity |
| Bride | Father of the Bride | Mother-In-Law |
| Best Friend | Bridesmaid | Maid of Honor |
| Church | Las Vegas | Hotel |
| Shower | Rehearsal Dinner | Anniversary |
| First Date | Going Steady | Engaged |
| Gifts | Wrapping Paper | Registry |
| D.J. | Justice of the Peace | Wedding Coordinator |
| Vacation | Honeymoon | Resort |
| Guests | Reception | Party Favors |
| Limousine | Chauffer | Red Carpet |
| Family | Ex-Girlfriend | Stepchildren |
| Beads | Lace | Silk |

| Level 1 | Level 2 | Level 3 |
| --- | --- | --- |
| Diamond | Gold | Engagement Ring |
| Cupid | Blind Date | Matchmaker |
| Birth Control | Children | Motherhood |
| Invitations | Guest Book | Thank You Cards |
| Rice | Garter Belt | Bouquet |
| Champagne | Speeches | Best Man |
| Games | Strippers | Bachelorette Party |
| Tuxedo | Black Tie | Formal |
| Photographer | Album | Posing |
| Cake | Bartender | Hors d'oeuvres |
| Friends | Love | Celebrate |
| Boyfriend | Fiancé | Husband |
| Bible | Vows | Holy Matrimony |
| Music | Limbo | First Dance |
| Witnesses | Blood Test | Marriage Certificate |
| Marriage | Tying the knot | Getting Hitched |

# THEME IDEAS - For Bachelorette Parties

There are many ways that you can spice up your bachelorette party. Listed below are several popular theme, entertainment, and transportation ideas for your special night out on the town.

**Dressing For The Occasion**
- Encourage guests to wear old bridesmaid dresses to the party.
- Encourage guests to dress up as their favorite Las Vegas entertainers.
- Throw a five-dollar formal where guests are encouraged to wear their "finest" evening wear. The only catch is that an outfit cannot cost more than five dollars.

As incentive to dress up and participate, we encourage you to offer a door prize for the best costume. Also, if you hire a stripper for the evening, let him know about the theme as he may be able to tailor his outfit or performance to accommodate the theme.

**Design a Collage**
- Encourage guests to bring a picture of themselves with the bachelorette, or others at the party, to add to a collage for the bride-to-be.
- Take magazine couples engaged in a variety of activities and paste the bride and grooms pictures over their faces. The pictures can be assembled into a collage or small photo album to document the couple's courtship. Fun captions can also be added to detail their adventures together.

## The Cure for the Common Stripper
## (A.K.A. Other Naughty Ideas)

- Ask party guests to purchase something racy (that they would actually use) and bring it to the party. This may include a pair of naughty underwear, furry handcuffs, lingerie, adult movies, etc. If the bachelorette correctly identifies who brought an item, then she keeps it.
- Buy a penis cake. This can be especially entertaining if you are starting the evening at a nice restaurant, and the wait staff agrees to serve the cake. Keep in mind, it is traditional to make the bachelorette take the first bite without the use of her hands!
- Buy a set of racy male playing cards to be distributed to the party guests. When you all go out, each guest searches for real men to match her cards. When a match is found, the man should autograph the card.

## The Cure for the Common Limo
## (A.K.A. Other Transportation Options)

- Rent a school bus, Winnebago/camper for the evening.
- "Borrow" the best man or several groomsmen as designated drivers for the evening.

# GETTING TIPSY

# I NEVER

**Number of Players** 6+

**Supplies**
- A full beverage per player

**Play**

Players sit in a circle and one is selected to go first. To begin the game, Player One thinks of something that she has never done. She then reveals it to the group. An example is, "I've never cheated on an exam." All of the players who have done this, must take a drink. If nobody in the group has ever cheated on an exam, then Player One must take a drink.

After players have taken their assigned drinks, the player to the right of Player One takes her turn.

There are three restrictions regarding the content of I Never statements:
I Never statements should be limited to one sentence.
I Never statements must be true.
I Never statements cannot be repeated.

Play continues for several rounds or until the participants are ready for a new adventure.

# TWO TRUTHS AND A LIE

**Number of Players**  2+

**Supplies**
- A piece of paper (for keeping score)
- A pen or pencil
- A full beverage per player

**Play**

Player One tells the other players three things about herself. Two of the statements should be true and one should be false. Statements may describe a player's opinions, feelings, aspirations, or memorable events. Players are encouraged to use statements based on beliefs or stories that they have not previously disclosed to other players. An example of a false statement might be, "Last week Hef called to offer me the June centerfold, but I turned him down since I did not want to miss this party." Whereas an example of a true statement might be, "I had to miss *Touched by an Angel* to be here tonight."

After Player One has announced her three statements, the player to her left guesses which statement is false. Guessing proceeds in a clockwise direction until all players have wagered a guess. Player One then reveals her false statement. Whoever guessed incorrectly takes a drink. After all players have taken a turn as the statement maker, begin Round Two. Play continues until you are ready for a different activity.

# THE MARITAL QUIZ

**Number of Players**  2+

*In preparation for this game, the hostess must quiz the groom-to-be on whether the descriptive statements listed in the Marital Quiz apply more to him or the bachelorette. For each question, the hostess records his answer (i.e., the appropriate name). This information should not be shared with the bachelorette prior to playing this game.*

*Note: Bonus questions have been included to test the groom's knowledge of his wife-to-be. Collect answers to these questions as well.*

**Supplies**
- A full beverage per player

**Play**

The hostess begins the game by asking a Marital Quiz question of the bachelorette. If the bachelorette's answer is the same as her fiancé's, the party guests must each take a drink. If she answers the question differently, the bachelorette must take a drink before proceeding to the next question. For bonus round questions, the bachelorette must take two drinks for each incorrect answer that her fiancé supplied. No drinks are assigned when the bachelorette and her fiancé give the same answer during the bonus round.

Play continues until the all of the questions have been asked.

## MARITAL QUIZ QUESTIONS

1. Who craves sex more? _____
2. Who is more likely to vote? _____
3. Who is more likely to call in sick to work? _____
4. Who is more likely to adopt a stray pet? _____
5. Who is more likely to hold a grudge? _____
6. Who is more competitive? _____
7. Who spent more time in detention? _____
8. Who has better manners? _____
9. Who is more likely to have a midlife crisis? _____
10. Who needs more mothering when sick? _____
11. Who has experimented more sexually? _____
12. Who wears the pants in the family? _____
13. Who is more open-minded? _____
14. Who is more likely to get a parking ticket? _____
15. Who is more likely to go to church? _____
16. Who is a worse backseat driver? _____
17. Who is more likely to have a freeloading relative? _____
18. Who is more likely to correct bad grammar? _____
19. Who is more likely to go skinny-dipping? _____
20. Who is more likely to do volunteer work? _____

### Bonus Round:
1. What is the bachelorette's favorite movie? _____
2. Who does she think is the sexiest Hollywood actor? _____
3. Which of the bachelorette's friends is the wildest? _____
4. Where would she go on her dream vacation? _____
5. When did you realize you wanted to marry her? _____

# MOST LIKELY

**Number of Players** 4+

**Supplies**
- A full beverage per player

**Play**

Players sit in a circle. Player One begins the game by asking a Most Likely question. Most Likely questions are posed to the entire group and should ask who the players think is most likely to carry out an action or behave a certain way. A list of Most Likely questions follows this game.

After asking the first question, Player One gives the other players time to decide on their answers. Then, starting to the left of Player One, the other players announce who they have chosen. Answers are limited to people playing the game and a player may choose herself. The person who asked the question keeps track of the votes. The player who receives the most votes is assigned a drink for each vote and then poses the next question. If two or more players tie, they both have to drink and the player who posed the original question asks the next question.

Play continues until the guest of honor has won the vote four times.

# SAMPLE MOST LIKELY QUESTIONS

1. Which player has the oddest music tastes?
2. Who is the biggest gossip?
3. Who is most likely to have cybersex?
4. Who is most likely to be arrested for indecent exposure?
5. Which player will have the most lovers in her old age?
6. Which player has the poorest eating habits?
7. Who do you suppose looks the best with her clothes off?
8. Which player would survive the longest if everyone were stranded on a deserted island?
9. Who is most likely to fall asleep while making love?
10. Which player would make the best talk show hostess?
11. Which player is most likely to own a gun?
12. Which player most needs a maid?
13. Who is most likely to end up in jail?
14. Which player would have the most inspiring biography?
15. Who is likely to have the most children?
16. Who do you suppose has the largest lingerie collection?
17. Which player is most likely to switch careers in the next couple months?
18. Which player do you believe would be the most demanding boss?
19. Which player would make the best gubernatorial candidate?
20. Who is likely to complain the most if the group was forced to play this game for another three hours?

# PERSONAL TRIVIA

**Number of Players** 8+

**Supplies**
- One hat (or bowl) per team
- One strip of paper per player
- Several pens or pencils
- A full beverage per player

**Setup**
One of the players, typically the hostess of the party, emcees the game. Players divide themselves evenly into two teams of four or more players.

Each player writes a true experience on a piece of paper. Players should choose personal experiences that have not been previously revealed to players on the other team. An example of an entry is "I used to be a phone sex operator." Players should not write their names on their entries or reveal their entries to the players on other teams. Completed entries should be folded and placed in their team's hat. After all players have submitted entries, the teams switch hats.

**Play**
The emcee draws an entry from Team One's hat. She reads the entry aloud, then Team One attempts to guess which player on

Team Two wrote the entry. The team can discuss the entry, but should provide an agreed-upon answer soon after the emcee reads it. The player who Team One guesses then reveals whether or not she wrote the entry. (If she did not write it, the true author should not be revealed but the entry is still discarded.) If Team One guesses correctly, every member on Team Two takes a drink. If Team One guesses incorrectly, every member of Team One takes a drink. Next, Team Two draws an entry and attempts to guess which player on Team One submitted it.

Teams continue taking turns drawing entries and wagering guesses until both teams' hats are empty. The team whose members have had to drink the least are the winners of this game.

**Variation**
Players may agree to raise the wager for certain types of trivia. For example, entries that are about sexual experiences could be worth two drinks.

# BAR DICE

**Number of Players** 6+

**Supplies**
- A single die
- A full beverage per player

**Play**

Players gather in a circle, and one is selected to go first.
Players take turns rolling the die. Based on the value that is
rolled, the players must perform the corresponding action
described below.

Roll Assignments:
- If you roll a one, then take one drink.
- If you roll a two, then assign one drink to any player.
- If you roll a three, the Bachelorette takes a drink.
- If you roll a four, select a letter of the alphabet and players
  take turns listing items related to a wedding that begin with
  that letter. Play begins with the roller and proceeds to her
  right. Play continues until a player is unable to think of an
  original word or phrase. The round is also terminated when
  a player repeats an item given by another player or fails to
  give her answer in a timely manner (within ten seconds).
  Whichever player terminates the round must take a drink.

- If you roll a five, then you may choose a category. Players take turns listing items in that category. An example of a category is alcoholic drinks starting with the letter M. Play begins with the roller and proceeds to her right. In this case she may start the round by saying, "Margarita." The next player might then say, "Martini." Play continues until a player is unable to think of an original word or phrase that fits the category. The round also ends when a player repeats a word given by another player or fails to give her answer in a timely manner (within ten seconds). Whichever player ends the round must take a drink.
- If you roll a six, you may ask a probing question of any player. If the player answers the question, then you must take a drink. If she refuses, she must take two drinks.

Play continues for five rounds or until the participants are ready for a new adventure.

# QUEEN ALMIGHTY

**Number of Players** 6+

## Supplies
- A deck of cards
- A large cup
- A full beverage per player

## Setup
Players sit around a table. For the first round, the guest of honor is the Queen Almighty and she assigns the other roles to players of her choice. One other player is the King, and a third is the Jester. The rest of the players are peasants. The King sits to the left of the Queen and the Jester sits to her right. The peasants sit wherever the Queen tells them to sit.

The Queen assigns one of the peasants to prepare the game. This peasant rinses out a large cup and places it in the center of the table. Then she shuffles the cards and spreads them out facedown around the center cup.

## Play
The Queen takes the first turn by turning over one of the facedown cards. The appropriate action is taken, then the King takes the next turn. Play continues around the table until the fourth ace is drawn.

The appropriate actions for each type of card that can be drawn are as follows:

Ace: Players who draw the first, second, or third ace, pour as much of their drinks into the center cup as they wish. The player who draws the fourth ace drinks the contents of the center cup and the round ends.

King: The King assigns someone to take a drink. If the Queen vetoes this drink assignment, then the King must drink.

Queen: The Queen assigns someone to take a drink. This can be one, several, or even all of the players.

Jack: The Jester must tell a joke. If no one laughs, she takes a drink.

10: The person drawing the card performs a hand or facial gesture, and everyone else must copy it. The last person to copy it is assigned the number of drinks the Queen wishes to bestow on her.

9: The player drawing the card tells a story about the guest of honor. If the group is not entertained, she takes a drink.

7: This card serves as protection from a drink assignment. A player drawing this card should hold onto it until she elects not to fulfill a drink assignment. At this point, the player plays the card and the Queen must take the assigned drink(s). A player can hold onto a '7' and use it if she draws the fourth Ace. In this case, the Queen would have to drink the center drink.

2-6, 8: The player drawing the card assigns a drink to a peasant.

## Establishing Rank

When you draw the first King, Queen, or Jack, take the appropriate action and keep the card. Whichever player draws the second or third of these cards collects the previously drawn cards of that type. For example if you draw the third Queen, collect the other two Queens and place all three of them in front of you. If you draw the fourth King, Queen, or Jack, the cards remain with you and you will be assigned that ranking for the next round. If you draw the fourth Ace, you drink the center drink. The round ends and also ranking is established for the next round of play. The person who drew the last Queen is the new Queen, the person who drew the last King is the new King, and the person who drew the last Jack is the new Jester. If a player has two or three sets of face cards, she can select the rank of her choice and assign the other rank(s) to whomever she chooses.

Everyone except the new Queen takes a drink to celebrate the new Queen. Then the Queen assigns a peasant to prepare for the next round. All the cards are then reshuffled and spread out facedown on the table around the center cup.

## Extra Drinks

The Queen or King may assign drinks to any peasant or the Jester at any time. The Jester can assign drinks to a peasant only if permission is granted by the Queen. Also, the Queen can overrule the King's drink assignments and can tell the King to do whatever she wishes.

# DRINK IDEAS

One of the best ways to celebrate your guest of honor is to "honor" her with special shots and cocktails. Listed below are recipes for drinks that will surely give your guest of honor a night she can only hope to remember:

**Shooters**

Sour Puss
Ingredients:     1 oz. Vodka
                 1/2 oz. Apple Pucker

Blow Job*
Ingredients:     1/2 oz. Kahlua
                 1/2 oz. Irish Cream
                 Top with Whipped Cream

* Your guest of honor must take the shot with both of her
   hands behind her back.

Slutty Redhead
Ingredients:     1/3 oz. Jagermeister
                 1/3 oz. Peach Schnapps
                 1/3 oz. Cranberry Juice

Brain Hemorrhage
                 1 1/4 oz. Light Rum
                 1/4 oz. Bailey's Irish Cream (add slowly)
                 3 drops Grenadine (in center, to look like blood)

# Cocktails

Creamy Sex on the Beach

Ingredients:    1 oz. Vodka
                3/4 oz. Chambord
                3/4 oz. Peach Schnapps
                Splash of Cranberry Juice
                Splash of Orange Juice
                Splash of Pineapple Juice
                Top with Whipped Cream

Flaming Orgasm*

Ingredients:    12 oz. Lager or Light Beer
                1 1/2  oz. Bacardi 151 Proof Rum

* Carefully light the shot, drop it into the Beer, then drink

Hard Banana

Ingredients:    1 oz. Vodka
                1 oz. Banana Liqueur
                Fill with Orange Juice

Follow the Rainbow

Ingredients:    1 oz. vodka
                1/2 oz. Apple Pucker
                Fill close to top with Sour Mix
                Splash of Blue Curacao
                Splash of Melon Liqueur
                Splash of Grenadine

# OUT ON THE TOWN

# KISS THE PIG

**Number of Players**  3+

*These instructions are to be read only by the hostess, since the object of the game is to trick participants into performing embarrassing acts.*

## Setup

Instruct the guest of honor that she must round up a group of men to participate in this game. She then gathers enough men so that everyone can sit at a table with members of the opposite sex on both sides (i.e., boy-girl-boy-girl).

The hostess explains to the group that she has an imaginary pig in her hands that she will be passing around. She instructs participants to kiss the imaginary pig someplace on its body, and then pass it to the left.

## Play

The hostess begins the game by announcing, "I kiss the pig on the (she chooses a body part)." She kisses the imaginary pig in the specified region, then hands it to the next player.

Participants are not allowed to name a body part that has already been selected by another player. Players continue selecting body parts and kissing them until the pig is returned to the hostess. The hostess then announces the instructions for the second round of the game. Everyone must now kiss the players to their lefts in the same specific regions that they kissed the imaginary pig. The hostess places the first kiss on the player to her left, and kissing continues around the circle. The round ends when the hostess receives a kiss from the player to her right.

## Variation

Instead of having everyone kiss the players on their left, you could have them all kiss the guest of honor.

# MANHUNT (A Scavenger Hunt)

**Number of Players**  4+

## Supplies
- A stopwatch (or clock)
- A pen or pencil

## Setup
Tear out or photocopy the Manhunt Challenge List that follows this game.  Make sure you are in a location where the guest of honor can approach strangers to assist her in completing the list.

## Play
The guest of honor must find different men to help her fulfill each of the challenges on the list.  Other guests may offer assistance in locating men for the deeds, but further assistance is not permitted.

At least one other woman must witness each act for it to be valid.  The bachelorette has two hours to complete all items on the list in any order she wishes.  If she fails to complete the list during the course of the evening, the other guests may devise a suitable penalty.  For example, if your guest of honor is a bachelorette, you could threaten to make her complete the scavenger hunt at her wedding reception.

# MANHUNT CHALLENGE LIST

1. Do a dirty dance with a younger man.

2. Have a (different) guy show you each of the following:

   a) A hidden body piercing.
   b) A tattoo.
   c) His tighty-whities.
   d) His G-string.
   e) A picture of his wife and kids.

3. Do a shot with a stranger.

4. Find three contestants for a best rear-end contest and award the winner with a kiss.

5. Approach a stranger with the following pickup line, "If I told you you had a beautiful body, would you hold it against me?"

6. Find a man who will give you a condom out of his wallet.

7. Find a stranger to describe his most recent sexual encounter to you.

# BODY SHOT RACES

**Number of Players**  6+

*We recommend that this game be played at a friendly neighborhood bar or a similar establishment. The game may result in loud raucous behavior (so make sure that the setting is appropriate). You will need to get two men at the bar to participate.*

## Supplies
- One shot of tequila (or other beverage) per player, extras may be required
- One lime wedge per player, extras may be required
- Two salt shakers

## Setup
Players divide themselves evenly into two teams. Each team must locate a man at the bar to act as the "body" for the race. The two bodies remove their shirts and sit in chairs next to each other. Each man should be given a salt shaker.

Players line up in front of their team's body. Each player should be given a tequila shot and a wedge of lime.

Note: You may wish to place an extra shot and lime next to each body, to be used if a player has to redo her turn.

**Play**

One of the players says "go," and the first player in each line approaches her team's body. The tequila shot should be placed between the man's legs, the man should then pour some salt anywhere on his torso or neck, and place the lime wedge in his mouth (with the rind facing inward). When the men are ready, the two shot-takers lick the salt off the bodies, quickly and carefully get to their knees and take the shot (without using their hands) and then bite the lime wedges out of the men's mouths. If a shot-taker does not drink at least half of the poured shot, she must redo her turn.

After the shot is completed, the team's body replaces the salt and the next player in line appropriately positions her lime and shot glass. Then she takes her shot. Play continues until all players successfully consume a body shot.

The team that completes all of its body shots first wins the game.

# WHO HAVE YOU DONE?

**Number of Players** 5+

## Supplies
- A stopwatch (or clock)
- A pen or pencil

## Setup
Tear out or photocopy both of the following two lists for the guest of honor to complete. Make sure you are in a location where she can approach strangers for answers.

## Play
The guest of honor has fifteen minutes to find people to sign their names next to an item on her first list that describes someone they have slept with. She may approach other party guests but at least half of the signatures must be from strangers. Each person can only sign the list once and the guest of honor cannot sign the list herself.

If she does not finish the first list in fifteen minutes, then she starts over with the second list. If she still fails, she must call her most conservative family member and explain why she was unsuccessful.

## WHO HAVE YOU DONE LIST - Innocent Version

Locate other people who have had sexual relations with the following types of people:

Someone Who is Ten+ Years Older _____

Someone Who is Ten+ Years Younger _____

A Teacher or Instructor _____

A Virgin _____

A Co-worker or Boss _____

A Stranger You Picked Up at a Bar _____

Two Other People at the Same Time _____

A Bald Man _____

A Family Friend _____

Someone Who Later Decided She (or He) was Gay _____

## WHO HAVE YOU DONE LIST – Naughty Version

Locate people who have had sexual relations with the following types of people:

Your Babysitter, Camp Counselor, or Tutor _____

Someone with an STD _____

A Famous Person _____

A Friend of a Current or Ex-Lover _____

Two Strangers (Separately) in One Evening _____

A Current or Ex-Lover of a Relative _____

A Member of the Same Sex _____

Someone with a Criminal Record _____

Someone Who was High on Drugs _____

A Married Couple _____

# THE RACE

**Number of Players** 8+

*This game is designed for the enjoyment of the guest of honor. While the teams hunt for men and fulfill the challenge list, the bachelorette can sit back and enjoy the fruits of their labor.*

## Supplies

- One list of actions per team
- One pen or pencil per team

## Setup

The hostess photocopies the attached List of Challenges for the party guests to accomplish throughout the course of the evening. Party guests are divided evenly into teams of three or more players (excluding the guest of honor), and the hostess distributes the copies immediately before play begins.

## Play

The teams must find different men who have engaged in specific actions, or who will help them fulfill each of the challenges found on the list following this game. Once they have done this, the volunteer must sign his name on the list next to the fulfilled challenge. At least one other woman must witness each act for it to be valid. The List of Challenges may be completed in any order.

Teams are awarded one point for each challenge that they successfully fulfill. Bonus points may also be earned to award truly outrageous behavior. Party guests must agree by majority that the act is worthy of a bonus point before the act is done.

The game ends when a team submits a complete list of challenges. Whoever has the most points at this time wins the game. If nobody completes the list of challenges, then the team with the most points at the end of the evening wins. If there is a tie, the guest of honor must either cast the deciding vote to determine the winning team or propose a final challenge to break the tie. Prizes should be awarded to members of the winning team.

## LIST OF CHALLENGES

1.  Locate a man who lives at home with his parents.
    Signature _____

2.  Locate a man who has served in the military for at least six
    years.  Signature _____

3.  Locate a man to buy a shot for the guest of honor.
    Signature _____

4.  Locate a man to serenade the guest of honor.
    Signature _____

5.  Locate a man who has at one time had a subscription to an
    adult magazine.  Signature _____

6.  Locate a man who is a vegetarian.
    Signature _____

7.  Locate a man to give the guest of honor a lap dance.
    Signature _____

8.  Locate a man who will give you a condom from his wallet.
    Signature _____

9.  Locate a man who has kissed/made out with another man.
    Signature _____

10. Locate a man with a tattoo with his ex-girlfriend's name in
    it.  Signature _____

11. Locate a man who has appeared in a television commercial
    or on the news.  Signature _____

12. Locate a man to passionately kiss the guest of honor.
    Signature _____

13. Locate a man who has dated a celebrity.
    Signature _____

14. Locate a man who goes to church regularly.

    Signature _____

15. Locate a man who will let the guest of honor give him a hickey. Signature _____

16. Locate a man to do a dirty dance with the guest of honor.

    Signature _____

17. Locate a man who has taken dance lessons.

    Signature _____

18. Locate a man who is not wearing any underwear.

    Note: this must be confirmed by the guest of honor!

    Signature _____

19. Locate a man who has modeled professionally.

    Signature _____

20. Locate a man who has earned a PhD.

    Signature _____

21. Locate a man who had traveled to at least four different continents. Signature _____

22. Locate a man who is a virgin.

    Signature _____

# DECORATING TIPS - for Bachelorette Parties

In this section we'd like to share with you ideas to assist you in decorating your bachelorette for her special night out. We recommend that you request assistance from other party guests so that you may use their artistic skills and creative minds to help you in the decorating process. We also recommend that you consider the bachelorette's comfort level when selecting appropriate decorations for her, so that the evening is enjoyable for all. Many of the items included on the following list can be made or easily purchased at party stores or online.

**Penis Straw**
The bachelorette must drink all of her drinks from this straw. This can be tied around the bachelorette's neck and worn as a necklace for the duration of the evening to ensure that she does not misplace it.

A fun variation of this is the penis pacifier that the bachelorette must carry for the duration of the evening.

**A Veil**
These can be fashioned using a tiara and mesh netting purchased at either an arts and crafts store or a costume store. You can supplement the veil by attaching foil decorations such as wedding bells, hearts, etc.

As an alternative, you may purchase a decorated tiara designed for bachelorette parties.

## A T-Shirt

A t-shirt can be designed to commemorate the event. A popular favorite is to sew pieces of candy to the shirt with an emblem stating "One Bite for a Buck" or "One Suck for a Buck". Men can then purchase a piece of candy to bite off of the t-shirt. Other options include fashioning the shirt with suggestive statements or creating t-shirts for each party guest to be worn when the group is out on the town.

## A Ball & Chain

A ball & chain can be purchased or made, and then secured to the bachelorette's ankle for the duration of the evening. A popular addition is to tape a picture of the groom to the ball.

## A Penis Bouquet

You may design a penis bouquet with several chocolate, candy, or plastic penises, tissue paper, and ribbon. This bouquet should accompany the bachelorette through her evening activities. A popular alternative is a penis corsage.

## A Risqué Outfit

You may design your own risqué outfit for the bachelorette to wear by requesting that each party guest bring a risqué item of clothing to decorate the bachelorette. This outfit can be supplemented with penis-shaped jewelry, noisemakers, squirt guns, etc. and custom-designed garters, sashes, boas, handcuffs and balloons.

## A Male Blow-up Doll

Another popular bachelorette party adventure is to handcuff a naked male blow-up doll to the bachelorette. It is her job to dress the dummy using clothing donated by men that she meets throughout the night.

## Party Favors

You may also supply the bachelorette with flavored or colored condoms, x-rated fortune cookies, or naughty candy to hand out to all of the wonderful men she meets throughout the night.

# DECORATING TIPS - for Birthdays

Decorating your guest of honor does not have to be a tradition solely for bachelorette parties. In this section, we'd like to share with you some entertaining, and sometimes embarrassing, ways to decorate your birthday girl.

## Balloons

What's a birthday party without balloons? Colorful, cartoon, and even tacky balloons are a great way to draw attention to your birthday girl.

## T-Shirts

There are many businesses on the internet and sometimes in shopping malls that will place a photograph on a t-shirt. Take your favorite photo of the birthday girl (perhaps a party photo where she looks a little tipsy) and print it on the back of a t-shirt. Underneath the photo you can print something to help encourage strangers in bars to give your birthday girl some attention, such as "I'm 30 today, buy me a drink!" or "Flash me, it's my birthday!"

## Fashion Accessories

There are many types of fashion accessories available at your local party and costume stores, such as birthday cake hats with candles, feather boas, tiaras, and magic wands. The first three ideas are just fun decoration ideas you can use to draw attention to your birthday girl, but the magic wand has an added bonus. The birthday girl could use the wand to get people to grant her birthday wishes.  This could include having people buy her drinks, kisses from attractive men, or special birthday treatment from waiters and bartenders.

## Subtle Decorations

One very easy and convenient decoration is to place bows or ribbons from birthday gifts in the birthday girl's hair or on her shirt.  Other subtle decorations include party streamer necklaces, bracelets, and anklets; confetti pasted to fingernails; candy necklaces; and gaudy Mardi Gras beads.

## Naughty Decorations

Yes, we know, "subtle" is not as fun as you can get.  If you want something more naughty, we have a few recommendations that will surely get your birthday girl to blush.  Get your birthday girl some unwanted attention at bars or clubs by placing a large hat on her head with a suggestive or embarrassing bumper sticker, like "So many men, so little time."  Types of hats that could be used include: a ten-gallon hat, a large sun hat, or one of those miner's helmets that holds two drinks and has built-in drink straws.  As an alternative, you could simply place a bumper sticker on the back of her shirt.   If you want to be really evil, write her age on a t-shirt and make her wear it out, or you can write her age on her cheeks with makeup.

# ROWDY AND RISQUÉ

# PSYCHOLOGY

**Number of Players**  6+

*These instructions should not be read or heard by the guest of honor. Ask her to go someplace where she cannot hear people talking before reading the rules aloud to the group.*

## Setup
The guest of honor leaves the room and players arrange themselves in a circle. The hostess then describes the secret of the game to the remaining players.

## Play
The secret of the game is that each player answers as if she were the player to her right. After the guest of honor returns, she will sit in the center of the circle and ask players personal questions until she figures out the secret of the game. Players should attempt to answer as truthfully as possible. If anyone recognizes that another player has given an incorrect answer, she should yell "Psychology!" Then all players stand up and scramble to find new seats in the circle.

The guest of honor should be encouraged to ask personal questions, not because it is a rule, but because it makes for a more interesting game.

There are a few rules that the guest of honor must follow when querying the other players:

- No asking about the significance of the word "Psychology".
- No asking about the reason for players switching chairs.
- No asking for clues or hints about the secret of the game.
- If the guesser wishes to make a guess about the secret of the game, it must be in the form of a yes/no question. For example, "Is the secret that everyone moves when a player laughs?" is acceptable.

If the guest of honor violates a rule, she should be assigned a shot of her favorite alcohol or liqueur.

The guest of honor may try to identify the secret of the game at any time. To win, she must identify that each player is answering as if she were the player to her right. Players should not let the guest of honor know how close she is to determining the secret. When the guest of honor identifies the secret, she wins the game and everyone may do a shot in her honor.

## Variation

If the guest of honor is unable to guess the secret in a reasonable amount of time, the group may appoint an assistant. The assistant (who knows the secret) joins the guesser in the center of the circle and takes over as the one who asks the questions. The assistant should ask questions that entertain the group, as well as ones that provide clues to the guest of honor about the game's secret.

# DIRTY DIARY

**Number of Players** 8+

## Supplies
- A pen or pencil

## Setup
Tear out or photocopy one of the Dirty Diary pages (following these game rules) and elect a person other than the bachelorette to be the reader of the Dirty Diary story.

## Play
The reader takes turns asking players missing words, including the bachelorette, to fill in the blanks in the story. When asking a player for a missing word, the reader should prompt whomever she asks by reading the information in parentheses under the missing word blank. The reader should not disclose details of the sentence or any other part of the story until after all the missing words have been added. Players should be encouraged to come up with creative descriptive words (e.g., green or filthy), actions (e.g., eat or copulate), body parts, items, ages, human characteristics (e.g., selfish or horny), etc.

The reader fills in the blanks with words provided by the players, then reads the story to the group once it is complete.

## DIRTY DIARY - A Love Story

Our dear, sweet bachelorette was not always so sweet.  Many
of you would be surpised to learn about her early days of

_____ debauchery.   In fact, when she was _____ ,
 (a descriptive word)                                      (an age)

her high school friends had nicknamed her _____ .

(a nickname)

She often got in _____ fights and even got kicked out of
          (an item)

school  for _____ a teacher.   It wasn't until she met
          (action ending in -ing)

her _____ husband-to-be that she started to settle
 (a descriptive word)

down.   When she first gazed into his _____ and noticed his
                                                        (body part)

intense _____ , she knew she had to change her ways.
    (human characteristic)

She stopped _____ every guy she met and she vowed
          (action ending in -ing)

never  to _____ again.   Now she is getting married
          (action, no -ing ending)

and we are very _____ for her.   Congratulations, your
                (emotion)

husband is one lucky son-of-a-_____ !
                              (swear word)

## DIRTY DIARY - Wedding Vows

The bride and groom have decided to write their own wedding
vows.  Our dear, sweet bachelorette is quite  _____
$$\phantom{x}$$
                                              (emotion)
about what she is writing, so let's help her.


My _____ husband:  you are my lover, my best friend
    (a descriptive word)
and most importantly the  _____ that I can always rely on.
                          (an item)
When we first met, I knew right then, I wanted to  _____
                                                   (action)
you and spend the rest of my life _____ by your side.
                                  (action ending in -ing)
Through _____ and through _____, I will always be
        (an event - plural)    (an event - plural)
with you, holding your _____ and _____ you.
                       (body part)      (action ending in -ing)
You are a beautiful _____ and  I will _____
                    (mammal)                    (emotion)
you for the rest of my _____ life.
                       (a descriptive word)

# PREPOSTEROUS PROPOSALS

## Number of Players  2+

## Supplies
- Paper, coins, or deck of cards
- A piece of paper (for keeping score)
- A pen or pencil
- A full beverage per player

## Setup
The hostess provides each player with two identical strips of paper. One piece should be marked with an 'A' for the first possible answer, and the other should be marked with a 'B' for the second possible answer. Nothing should be written on the reverse sides of the papers. Playing cards or coins may be substituted for the pieces of paper. If cards are selected, a red-suited card signifies a response of 'A' and a black-suited card signifies a response of 'B'. For coins, heads should represent 'A' and tails should represent 'B'.

## Play
Players take turns making Preposterous Proposals to one another. Each proposal must have only two possible answers to choose from (i.e., a yes/no question or a multiple choice question with only two options).

An example of a Preposterous Proposal is, "Who would you rather see naked?

A) Your favorite comedian

B) Your favorite singer"

A list of sample Preposterous Proposals follows this game.

Before the selected player reveals her answer, everyone else must try to predict her response based on an assessment of her character. To record their guesses, players should select the side of the paper, card, or coin which represents the anticipated response. They should be careful not to reveal their guesses to the other players. Once every player is ready, the recipient of the proposal reveals her answer. Keep in mind, the player's answer must be truthful! The other players then share their predictions with the group. Players who guess incorrectly take one drink.

# SAMPLE PREPOSTEROUS PROPOSALS

1. Would you take a job doing hair and makeup for funeral home residents for double your salary?
A) Yes
B) No

2. Which accomplishment would you prefer?
A) Being the highest paid model in the country
B) Being the first woman president of the United States

3. If you were a jury member for a high-profile celebrity trial, would you consider doing the talk show circuit?
A) Yes
B) No

4. If you were cast on a reality-based television show, which stereotypical character would you prefer to be known as?
A) The Bitch
B) The Slut

5. Which superhero would you rather date?
A) Batman
B) Spiderman

6. Which would you prefer to do?
A) Change an event that occurred in your past
B) Determine an event that will occur in your future

7. If you had to abolish either of the following, which would you choose?

A) Religion

B) Science

8. Which awards ceremony would you prefer to help choose the candidates for?

A) The Oscars

B) The Grammys

9. You were caught drawing graffiti on the walls of City Hall. What punishment would you rather be given?

A) 100 hours community service

B) One night in jail

10. What would you rather discover tomorrow?

A) Your ideal job to match your skills

B) Your ideal lover to fulfill your needs

11. What would you find more annoying?

A) A phone that never stops ringing

B) Tennis shoes that whistle when you walk

12. What would you be more willing to give up?

A) Television and Movies

B) All Cosmetic Products

13. Who would you rather kiss passionately?

A) Your most recent ex-lover

B) His father

14. Where would you rather spend the rest of this evening?

A) At a strip club

B) In bed with any two men of your choice

15. What would your rather suffer from?

A) Chronic hair loss

B) Compulsive gambling

16. What would you rather give up?

A) The ability to make love

B) Your sense of humor

17. Who would you rather take to prom?

A) Danny Zuko (John Travolta) from *Grease*

B) Johnny Castle (Patrick Swayze) from *Dirty Dancing*

18. When you get adventurous, what are you more likely to do?

A) Go skinny-dipping

B) Go sky diving

19. What would you rather pierce?

A) Your bellybutton

B) Your lover's tongue

# THAT'S DISGUSTING!

**Number of Players**  8

## Supplies
- Two chairs
- A hat (or bowl)
- A two-minute timer
- Eight strips of paper
- A pen or pencil

## Setup
There are eight topics for this game:

- Drunken adventures
- Sexual endeavors
- Insects and vermin
- Vomit
- Menstrual cycle
- Bodily fluids
- Blood and guts
- Rotting objects

One of the players, typically the hostess, emcees the game. She writes down the eight topics individually on the strips of paper.  She folds them, and places them in a hat.  The emcee then places two chairs at the front of the room and asks the guest of honor and a volunteer the guest of honor selects to sit in the chairs.

## Play

The emcee begins the first round by selecting one of the topics and presenting it to the guest of honor. The guest of honor has two minutes to think of the most disgusting story she can tell (that pertains to the topic presented). Before the two-minute preparation time elapses, she begins telling her story. The story must be true and she must be a main character in it. She has only two minutes to tell her story and should attempt to disgust the crowd as much as possible.

Next, the emcee selects a second topic and the second contestant has two minutes to prepare and then two minutes to tell her most disgusting true story (that pertains to the topic presented).

After both players have shared their stories on the topic, the emcee asks the audience to vote on the story that they found the most disgusting. The emcee names the contestants one by one and the members of the audience raise their hands after the name of their selected winner is called. If there is a tie, the guest of honor loses.

The next round begins. The guest of honor remains on stage and is joined by another guest selected by the previous volunteer. Each player tells her story, the audience votes, and the game continues until the guest of honor wins two rounds.

If the topics run out before the guest of honor wins two rounds, then the emcee tells the most disgusting story she knows involving the guest of honor as punishment, and the game ends.

# INDECENT PROPOSITIONS

**Number of Players**  5+

**Supplies**
- A piece of paper (for keeping score)
- Ten strips of paper per player
- One pen or pencil per player

**Setup**

One of the players, typically the hostess of the party, emcees the game.  In preparation for this game, she needs to develop a list of ten questions or she may use one of the sample question lists following this game.  The first sample list can be used for any type of party, the second list was designed strictly for bachelorette parties.

Each question on the Indecent Proposition lists asks how much the guest of honor would need to be paid to perform a certain unpleasant act.  An example is "How much would I have to pay you to be an exotic dancer for an evening?"

The emcee places three chairs at the front of the room and asks for three volunteers (other than the guest of honor).  She selects the players and they seat themselves in the chairs.

## Play

The hostess begins the game by asking the guest of honor the first question from her list. The guest of honor then considers how much financial incentive (money) it would require to get her to perform the unpleasant act that was presented to her. At the same time, the three players wager guesses by writing down how much money they think the guest of honor would have to be paid to perform the action. Any player or audience member can ask the emcee to elaborate on the question during this time. Consider the previous example question, "How much would I have to pay you to be an exotic dancer for an evening?" A player may want to know the job responsibilities of an exotic dancer. Players can adjust their answers accordingly after the emcee addresses any questions.

Once all three players have written down dollar amounts, the answers are final and no more questions may be asked. The guest of honor announces her answer. Then the players reveal their answers. The player who guesses the closest, without going over, scores a point. For example, if the guest of honor says $5,000, Player One guesses $10,000, Player Two guesses $3,000, and Player Three guesses $5,500, Player Two scores the point because Player One and Player Three both overbid. If all three players overbid, no one receives a point and the question is discarded. The emcee then poses a second question to the guest of honor.

The emcee continues asking questions until all ten questions have been answered. At this point, the emcee tallies the score and awards the prize to the player with the highest score. If there is a tie, the emcee should come up with a tie-breaking question. The person that scores the final point breaks the tie and wins the prize.

## SAMPLE INDECENT PROPOSITIONS

1. How much would I have to pay you not to shower for two weeks?
2. How much would I have to pay you to abstain from sex, alcohol, smoking, and caffiene for a month?
3. How much would I have to pay you to do a cameo in an erotic film?
4. How much would I have to pay you to flash your chest to your pizza delivery boy?
5. How much would I have to pay you to sing your favorite childhood song and let it be broadcast on your city's most popular radio station?
6. How much would I have to pay you to quit your job and join the Marines?
7. How much would I have to pay you to shave your head?
8. How much would I have to pay you to show up at your favorite dance club wearing your prom dress?
9. How much would I have to pay you to give up wearing deodorant forever?
10. How much would I have to pay you to apply for a job at a strip club?

# SAMPLE INDECENT PROPOSITIONS - Bachelorette Version

1. How much would I have to pay you not to open your wedding gifts, but instead donate them to charity?
2. How much would I have to pay you to abstain from sex on your honeymoon?
3. How much would I have to pay you to kiss every man you meet in the next twenty-four hours?
4. How much would I have to pay you to postpone your wedding and sign up for a reality game show?
5. How much would I have to pay you to contact an ex-boyfriend/ex-husband and ask him to "give you away" at your wedding?
6. How much would I have to pay you to wear your wedding dress every day for the next two weeks?
7. How much would I have to pay you to come down the aisle on roller skates?
8. How much would I have to pay you to show up at your wedding going commando (i.e., not wearing underwear)?
9. How much would I have to pay you to get a tattoo with your fiancé's name?
10. How much would I have to pay you to spank your inlaws at your wedding reception?